A History of

Italy

Through Art

Nathaniel Harris

Wayland

Titles in this series

A History of Britain through Art

A History of France through Art

A History of Italy through Art

A History of the United States of America through Art

Cover: *Pope Alexander Gives a Spear to Doge Ziani* by Spinello Aretino
Title page: Detail from *Good Government in the City* by Ambrogio Lorenzetti

Series Editor: Rosemary Ashley
Book Editor: Joanne Jessop
Designer: Jean Wheeler

First published in 1995 by Wayland (Publishers) Limited
61 Western Road, Hove, East Sussex, BN3 1JD, England

© Copyright 1995 Wayland (Publishers) Limited

British Library Cataloguing in Publication Data
Harris, Nathaniel
History of Italy Through Art. – (History Through Art Series)
I. Title II. Series
945

ISBN 0-7502-1590-9

Typeset by Jean Wheeler
Printed and bound by L.E.G.O. S.p.A.,Vicenza, Italy

Acknowledgements
The Publishers would like to thank the following for allowing their pictures to be reproduced in this book:
AKG London title page 5, bottom, 17, 18, 20, 21, 29, 34, 41; Associated Press/Topham 45; The Bridgeman Art Library 11, 9, 23 (Bernard Cox), 25, 27, 33; C M Dixon 12, 13; e t archive cover, 7, 14, 30, 31, 37; Ronald Grant 42; Imperial War Museum 43; Tony Stone Worldwide 5 top (Oliver Benn), 19 (Doug Armand); Topham Picture Point 44; Visual Arts Library 38.

CONTENTS

The pictures in this book span over a thousand years of Italian history – from the last days of the Roman Empire to the present day. Until the 1860s Italy was a land divided into small states and dominated by foreign powers. In 1860, troops led by Garibaldi freed Sicily and landed on the Italian mainland to join forces from the north. Soon all of Italy was joined together as one nation. The various works of art show us some of the many events and experiences that have shaped the history of Italy.

ROME AND THE BARBARIANS

In ancient times, Italy lay at the centre of the great Roman Empire, which spread right around the Mediterranean Sea. But by the fourth century AD the empire was growing steadily weaker under the attacks of barbarian tribes from beyond its frontiers.

To make the defence of the Roman Empire easier, its vast territories were divided into two parts. One emperor ruled the West from Rome, while the other ruled the East from Constantinople (now Istanbul, in Turkey). Although the Romans had built the empire, Italy was no longer strong. Barbarian peoples invaded, and in AD 476 the last Roman emperor in the West was forced to give up his throne.

This is often described as 'the fall of the Roman Empire'. But in fact, the empire survived in the East for almost another thousand years. During this period, it is usually known as the Byzantine Empire.

Even in Italy, the story of the Roman Empire was not quite over. In 535 the Byzantine emperor, Justinian, recaptured Italy from the barbarians. Justinian ignored the once-great city of Rome and governed Italy from Ravenna, on the north-east coast. Mosaics (pictures made from tiny coloured stones) can still be seen in a Ravenna church (see opposite), glorifying Justinian and his empress, Theodora.

In 568, the Lombards, a new barbarian people, crossed the Alps and occupied northern Italy. The Byzantines held on to the South. Italy was now a divided land, and later became even more divided as different powers within the peninsula fought among themselves to gain control. Yet Italians never forgot how great Rome had once been, and the idea of creating a new Roman Empire remained alive.

The Colosseum in Rome ▶
This enormous arena, built in the first century AD, IS a powerful reminder of the achievements of the Roman Empire.

▼ *The Empress Theodora and her Attendants*
This is a mosaic in the Church of San Vitale, Ravenna.

POPES AND EMPERORS

The Italians had been Christians since the late Roman Empire. During the troubled times after the fall of the empire, the bishops of Rome, or popes, became strong leaders. Eventually the popes controlled the Church all over Europe.

The first bishop of Rome was St Peter, who had been made the head of the Christian Church by its founder, Jesus of Nazareth. So the popes, who followed Peter as bishops of Rome, could claim that his position as leader had been passed on to them. The claim was not accepted everywhere, but by the sixth century the pope was recognized all over western Europe as the head of the Church.

However, when Pope Leo III got into difficulties with the Lombards, he was rescued by the powerful king of the Franks, Charlemagne. Leo was so grateful that, on Christmas Day 800, he crowned Charlemagne emperor of what became known as the Holy Roman Empire. After Charlemagne's death, there were new troubles in Europe again. Muslim Arabs, or Saracens, captured the large Italian island of Sicily, and savage Magyar tribesmen raided the north of the country. Then, in 951, the German king, Otto I, crossed the Alps and defeated the Magyars, who settled down in what is now Hungary. Once again the pope crowned a northern conqueror as emperor, and after this the German kings expected to hold the title of Holy Roman Emperors.

In the years that followed, emperors and popes began to quarrel about who should have the most power. The emperors seemed stronger, but they found it hard to control both Germany and northern Italy, especially since many Italian nobles and cities preferred to be independent and sided with the popes. Also, the popes often used their religious authority against the emperors.

Pope Alexander Gives a Spear to Doge Ziani

by Spinello Aretino (c.1350–1410). This wall painting is in the City Hall, Siena.

The popes often waged war on the Holy Roman Emperors by making alliances with other rulers.

◀ The spear is a symbol of power and strength. By handing it to the Doge, who ruled Venice, Pope Alexander was giving his blessing to a war waged by the Doge against the Holy Roman Emperor, Frederick I.

THE RISE OF THE CITIES

By about AD 1000, Europe was recovering from centuries of barbarian invasions. Trade was increasing and the cities were growing. But the cities in Italy grew much faster than those in the rest of Europe, and a new, city-based kind of society developed.

One of the main reasons for the rapid rise of Italian cities was the geographical position of Italy, in the south of Europe, thrusting out into the Mediterranean Sea. Ports around the Italian coast were on the main trade route from east to west. Goods from the East naturally passed through Italy on their way to Europe. So did goods going in the other direction. Italians became important carriers of goods, traders and, in time, bankers. As a result, dozens of great cities grew up in Italy. Ports such as Venice, Genoa and Pisa built large fleets and even set up colonies outside Italy. Milan, Florence and many other cities developed and grew rich on overland trade routes. The Italians also became manufacturers, building up a huge, internationally important cloth industry.

The wealthy northern Italian cities wanted to manage their own affairs, and they fought to free themselves from the control of local bishops and nobles. Many cities were supposed to obey the Holy Roman Emperor, but the quarrels between emperors and popes (see page 6) gave them the chance to become independent. Some cities conquered the territories around them, expanding until they became small states, known as city-states.

The city-states constantly fought one another. Inside each city, too, there were usually two parties – the Guelfs (supporters of the pope) and the Ghibellines (supporters of the emperor) – who often battled with each other. Surprisingly, Italy thrived in spite of all these conflicts.

▼ *Good Government in the City* by Ambrogio Lorenzetti (c.1290–1348). This wall painting is in the City Hall, Siena.

◀ The people here are able to enjoy themselves because they live under a good government. Another painting by Lorenzetti in the same room shows the misery caused by bad government. Italians in the fourteenth century were already giving careful attention to political problems.

THE CHURCH IN ITALY

During the Middle Ages (c.1000–1400), most people in Europe belonged to the Christian Church. So the leaders of the Church, the popes, became powerful throughout Europe. As well as great popes, Italy also produced many saints and religious thinkers.

An important early churchman was St Benedict (c.480–c.550), who founded the famous Italian monastery of Monte Cassino in about 529. The rules drawn up by Benedict were followed by monasteries all over the West, and for several centuries all Christian monks were Benedictines.

There were many remarkable popes, but not all of them were Italian. A French pope, Urban II, called on Christians to recover the holy city of Jerusalem from the Muslims, followers of the religion of Islam. The pope's preaching was so effective that a great army was raised and set out in 1096 to fight the Muslims. This expedition, called the first Crusade, was a success.

During this period, the pope's authority steadily increased. For a time, Pope Innocent III (1198–1216) seemed able to make or break emperors and kings. But then things went wrong. Between 1305 and 1378 the popes even left Italy and lived at Avignon, under the protection of the powerful French king. Then, during 'the Great Schism' (division), which lasted from 1378 to 1417, the Church was split between rival churchmen, each claiming to be the true pope. The scandal ended when a Church council chose a new pope.

▲ Giotto's lively painting of birds and trees reflected a new interest artists were showing in the world around them.

Fortunately, Italy also produced more worthy religious figures. St Thomas Aquinas (c.1225–74) was the greatest Christian philosopher of the Middle Ages. St Francis of

Assisi (c.1181–1226) was the most loved and admired of saints, famous for his great love of all creatures and of nature. St Francis founded the Franciscan order of friars; his female follower, St Clare, founded the order of nuns known as the Poor Clares.

St Francis Preaching to the Birds by Giotto (1266–1337). The picture is painted on a wall in the Church of San Francesco (St Francis) in Assisi.

SOUTHERN ITALY AND SICILY

Southern Italy and Sicily developed in a different direction from the north. Instead of becoming separate city-states, the south was united into a single powerful kingdom. But after a period of glory, the region became poor and backward.

Norman knights
These figures are carved on the capitals (tops) of columns in Monreale Cathedral, Sicily. They show the medieval conquerors of the island in action.

In the ninth century, Sicily was conquered by the Arabs, who brought with them the religion of Islam and an advanced civilization. The mainland of southern Italy was divided among Arabs, Byzantines and Lombards. Then, from about 1050, Norman adventurers, from northern France, gradually conquered the south and Sicily. Their state, known as the Kingdom of Sicily, became very strong and wealthy.

The Norman kings were followed by Frederick II (1194–1250), who ruled Germany as Holy Roman Emperor as well as being the king of Sicily. Frederick was a brilliant man; his court at Palermo became a great centre of culture, and he was described by admirers as 'The Wonder of the World'. Frederick waged constant wars in Italy, which was again divided between Guelfs and Ghibellines. But in the long run he had no more success than earlier emperors in gaining control over the whole country.

Frederick's son, Manfred, looked as though he might be able to conquer all of Italy. So the pope called in a French prince, Charles of Anjou, who defeated Manfred and became the new king of Sicily. But the French were unpopular rulers, and Sicily broke away after a revolution called the Sicilian Vespers (1282). The southern mainland became the Kingdom of Naples. For centuries to come, Sicily belonged to the Spanish kingdom of Aragon.

In spite of their earlier wealth, the southern cities failed to keep up with the north. Wars, taxes and fighting among the nobles helped to make the south of Italy poor and backward. The difference between north and south has lasted right down to the present day.

An Arab fountain in Sicily
This fountain, at the Christian Cathedral at Monreale, Sicily, reminds us that Arabs conquered Sicily in the ninth century, and that many remained on the island for centuries after Christian forces reconquered it. The Arabs brought with them new ideas and skills of great value.

THE MERCHANTS OF VENICE

For a long time, the most successful city-states were those on the Italian coast. Amalfi, Pisa and Genoa, on the west coast, and Venice on the east (Adriatic) coast all had great fleets and grew rich from trade. But these city-states were bitter enemies, always at war with each other.
Finally Venice became the supreme trading sea power.

Venice was founded by people who fled from the mainland during the barbarian invasions and settled on some swampy islands off the north-east coast. Over the years, they built up the islands, bridging the waters between them. Eventually Venice became an unusual but beautiful city in which most of the 'streets' were actually canals – as they still are today.

One important reason for the success of Venice was its very stable government. It was an independent republic with an elected head known as the Doge. Power was held by a small number of families, but they usually served the state well. Unlike the other Italian city-states, Venice avoided civil wars and revolutions.

Most of Venice's wealth came from its trade with the East. Venetian ships brought in luxuries such as spices and silks, which were sent over the mountain barrier of the Alps and sold in northern Europe for high prices. To protect their route to the East, the Venetians seized islands and coastal lands all along the eastern Mediterranean.

The most famous Venetian traveller was Marco Polo. He left for the East in 1271, lived in China and travelled over much of Asia. No other European had done anything like it. After his return in 1295, Marco was captured in a war between Venice and Genoa. He passed the time in prison by dictating the story of his travels to a fellow-prisoner. The book became famous all over Europe, although Marco's stories seemed so fantastic that at first people thought he had made them all up!

▲ Venetian ships carried travellers and goods back and forth along the Mediterranean Sea. As well as big sails, they had many oars, so they could make progress by rowing even when there was no wind.

◀ *Marco Polo sets out from Venice*
This is an illustration painted in a book that is now kept in the Bodleian Library, Oxford.

FLORENCE AND THE MEDICI

Florence was probably the liveliest and most creative of all the Italian city-states. It was at its most brilliant during the fifteenth century, under the rule of the Medici family.

The city of Florence lies in the region known as Tuscany. Florence conquered it neighbours and soon had all of Tuscany under its control. The Florentines were a hard-working people who became wealthy by manufacturing cloth from the wool they imported from other countries – some as far away as England. Later they became the first international bankers, establishing offices in many lands.

The Florentines were proud of their city, bravely defending it on many occasions. But, like other city-dwellers, they often fought among themselves. They split into Guelfs and Ghibellines, and when the Guelfs won, they split into two new Guelf parties – Blacks and Whites – which fought each other just as fiercely!

One victim of these troubles was the poet Dante Alighieri (1265–1321). Although Dante died in exile, his great work, *The Divine Comedy*, was so admired that its Florentine language became the main form of Italian speech.

During the fifteenth century, Florence produced many great statesmen, artists and thinkers. The city was filled with fine palaces and churches, and Florentines played a great part in the Renaissance (see page 18). Benozzo Gozzoli's painting gives us an idea of their wealth, pride and energy. It was painted to glorify the Medici family who ruled Florence. From 1436, Florence enjoyed peace and prosperity, first under the banker Cosimo de' Medici and then under his grandson, Lorenzo the Magnificent.

The Journey of the Magi
by Benozzo Gozzoli (c.1421–97). This is a wall
painting in the Medici Palace in Florence.

The subject of this painting is religious – the journey
of the Wise Men to see the new-born Jesus at
Bethlehem. But in reality it is just an excuse for
glorifying Florence's ruling family, the Medici.

THE ITALIAN RENAISSANCE

The Renaissance was a great age of art, thought and action that lasted from about 1350 to 1600. Renaissance Italy produced some of the greatest geniuses in history. More important still, it changed the way people thought about the world and their place in it.

The School of Athens
by Raphael (1483–1520). A wall painting in the Vatican, Rome.

Raphael has imagined a gathering of ancient Greeks, but some are portraits of Renaissance artists.

During this period, Italian city life encouraged a new spirit of confidence in what human beings could achieve. People began to be more curious about the world around them and to look for new and better ways of doing things in art, literature, architecture and science. This new outlook appeared first in Italy and then spread much later to the rest of Europe.

The Italians of the Renaissance learned much from the ancient civilizations of Greece and Rome, and modelled themselves on its heroes. The artist Raphael, in his painting *The School of Athens*, imagined the famous Greek philosophers meeting and talking together. The picture shows us Raphael's admiration for the ancient Greeks and his noble view of human beings.

There were many famous Renaissance Italians. Cosimo and Lorenzo de' Medici governed Florence wisely. Cesare Borgia, the son of a pope, was a cruel leader who had a short, colourful and murderous period in power. Machiavelli was the first writer to describe politics realistically. Julius II was a famous warrior pope. Even Christopher Columbus, the first European to open up the New World, was an Italian in the pay of Spain.

Renaissance Italy is probably best known for the new developments that took place in painting, sculpture, architecture and science. Italian artists celebrated human greatness and the world around them. The most famous of the many outstanding artists were Leonardo da Vinci, Michelangelo, Raphael and Titian.

A view of Florence
Looming over the skyline in this photograph is the great dome of the Cathedral, designed by the Florentine architect Filippo Brunelleschi (1377–1446). It was a great feat of engineering – probably the biggest dome to be built since ancient times. On the right stands the tower of the Old Palace, from which Florence was governed.

THE RISE AND FALL OF SAVONAROLA

After a long period of stability under the Medici, Florence found an unexpected new leader. For a few years, a reforming friar named Girolamo Savonarola dominated the city.

Girolamo Savonarola
by Fra Bartolommeo
(c.1472–1517). The portrait is in the Museum of San Marco, Florence.

Savonarola became well known in the early 1490s, when he began to preach against the sins of the Florentines. By this he meant their love of luxuries, beautiful clothes, books, pictures and other worldly (non-religious) things. Savonarola was a powerful speaker, and the thousands of people who went to hear his sermons were frightened when he warned of terrible times to come.

Savonarola's warnings seemed to come true when Lorenzo de' Medici died and his son Piero took over as leader. In 1494, Piero weakly handed over Florentine fortresses to the French army when they marched through Italy. The Florentines were so ashamed they drove Piero from power. Savonarola took over as the ruler of Florence.

Under Savonarola, holy days were marked with religious processions and fasting rather than carnivals. Many writers and artists became followers of Savonarola and brought their books and paintings, along with cosmetics and fine clothes, to be burned on a 'bonfire of vanities'.

But Savonarola made the mistake of speaking out against the pope, Alexander VI. Alexander was not a good pope, but he was a powerful enemy who condemned Savonarola and used his influence to damage Florence's trade. Soon the Florentines became tired of the hard times and stern way of life under Savonarola. He was arrested and tortured, and on 23 May 1498 he was hanged and burned in the main square of Florence.

The Death of Savonarola by an unknown artist who lived about the same time. It is in the Museum of San Marco, Florence.

THE ITALIAN WARS

Italians prided themselves on their mastery of the arts – including the art of war. But by the sixteenth century, a divided Italy was no match for its powerful neighbours.

By about 1400, Italy was dominated by five states – Milan, Venice, Florence, the Papal States in Central Italy (ruled directly by the pope), and the Kingdom of Naples in the south. No single state was strong enough to conquer the rest, so Italy remained divided.

Although other countries envied Italy's wealth, for most of the fifteenth century there were few serious threats from abroad. When two Italian states went to war, most of the fighting was done by mercenaries – professional soldiers who fought for pay and had no reason to kill one another. As a result, wars between the states usually involved clever tactics and quick deals rather than fights to the death.

But beyond the Alps, large and powerful nation states had grown up. In 1494, the French invaded Italy under King Charles VIII, who claimed the throne of Naples. Italians were shocked by the size and strength of Charles's army and realized, too late, how weak they were. It seemed that the only way they could resist an invader was with the help of another foreign power.

The disastrous result was that Italy became a battlefield between the leading European powers, and whichever of them won, Italy's independence would be lost. A thirty-year struggle between Francis I of France and Charles V, the Holy Roman Emperor and king of Spain, ended in victory for Charles. By 1559 the Spanish ruled Milan, Naples, Sicily and Sardinia, and dominated the rest of Italy.

The Colleoni Monument
by Andrea del Verrocchio
(1435–88).

This bronze sculpture, which
stands in a square in
Venice, portrays a
famous soldier who
served Venice.

POPES AND REFORMERS

By the end of the Middle Ages, many people were discontented with the behaviour of the popes and the condition of the Church. In northern Europe there was a serious revolt against the authority of the pope and the Catholic Church. In reply, the Church reorganized itself and fought back in a powerful movement that became known as the Counter-Reformation

In spite of the Great Schism (see page 10), the popes recovered their full authority over the Church. During the fifteenth century the popes were often remarkable men. Julius II (1503–13) began building St Peter's in Rome, which became the greatest church in the West. He employed Michelangelo, Raphael and other great artists to work on it. Even in old age, Pope Julius personally led his armies to war.

However, many people felt that popes should be more concerned with religion and less with fine buildings, art and war. Part of the trouble was that the pope was the ruler of an Italian state – and therefore a politician – as well as a religious leader. This brought disaster in 1527, when Pope Clement VII fought against the Holy Roman Emperor, Charles V. Charles's troops stormed Rome, plundering and killing. This 'Sack of Rome' was so horrific that it has often been seen as the end of the Renaissance.

Meanwhile, there was growing discontent with the way the Church was run and some of its teachings. In 1517 a German monk named Martin Luther (1483–1546) defied Pope Leo X. Eventually Luther, and other people who felt like him, formed their own Protestant churches in opposition to the Roman Catholic Church. These events are now known as the Protestant Reformation.

Few Italians became Protestants, but the Reformation attracted many followers in other European countries. Finally, the Catholic Church realized how seriously it was threatened by Protestantism. In Italy and elsewhere, a new religious spirit developed. At the Council of Trent, which met between 1545 and 1564, Church leaders tightened up the Church's teachings and practices. This began the Counter-Reformation, which greatly strengthened the Catholic Church and strongly affected life in Italy.

The Council of Trent
by Pasquale Cati (1550–1620). This painting is in the Church of Santa Maria in Trastevere, Rome.

The scene at the front is meant to be symbolic, showing the triumph of the Catholic Church.

UNDER FOREIGN RULE

Foreign powers controlled Italy for more than two centuries, often fighting their wars on Italian soil. Individual Italians continued to make important contributions in the arts and sciences, but their country was poor and backward.

Spain was the dominant foreign power in Italy until 1713, when the Spanish Empire was divided up. Then Austria replaced Spain, taking control of the north. During the seventeenth and eighteenth centuries there were many wars, and territories often changed hands.

The only truly independent Italian states were Piedmont and Venice. Piedmont lay in the north-west and could control the mountainous passes through the Alps that led into Italy. By choosing the right allies at the right time, Piedmont actually became larger and stronger during this period.

Venice, like most of Italy, was growing poorer. Italy was no longer on the main trade routes, which now crossed the Atlantic to the New World or went around Africa to the East. Bad government, destructive wars and heavy taxes made things worse, especially in the south.

During this period the stern mood of the Counter-Reformation made Italy a dangerous place for anyone who tried to think freely or disagreed with the Catholic Church. The scientist Galileo (1564–1642), for example, was arrested and forced to withdraw his argument that the earth moved round the sun because this theory was thought to conflict with the teachings of the Church.

In spite of its decline, Italy was greatly admired by people in other countries. The Italians were still a creative people; for example, they invented the art of opera, which spread

all over the Western world. People from all over Europe came to Italy to see the remains of ancient Rome and the glories of the Renaissance, and also to enjoy Italy's famous carnivals and masked balls. The painting by Gaspare Vanvitelli shows us what the eighteenth-century tourists saw when they visited Rome – both its mighty monuments and its rather run-down condition.

The River Tiber in Rome
by Gaspare Vanvitelli (1653–1736). It belongs to a private owner.

This sleepy view of the river is not what we expect to see in the middle of a great city like Rome.

NAPOLEON IN ITALY

The French Revolution of 1789 shook all of Europe. Italy was directly affected when the French army invaded, claiming to bring the country freedom. The short but spectacular career of the French leader, Napoleon Bonaparte, made a lasting impression on Italians.

During the Revolution, the French executed their king and set up a republic. The French Revolution was based on the ideals of liberty, equality and human rights, which were hated by the kings and nobles of Europe. Soon France was at war with almost all the other European states.

Italy remained quiet until 1796 when a brilliant French general, Napoleon Bonaparte (1769–1821), swept through the north and drove out the Austrians; Baron Gros's painting shows Napoleon during the battle of Arcola. Napoleon set up republics in Italy, but he showed his ruthlessness when he made peace with Austria in 1797. As part of the agreement, Venice was simply handed over to the Austrians, ending its thousand years of independence.

Having seized power in France, Napoleon made himself emperor in 1804. Then in 1805 he created the Kingdom of Italy in the north of the country, with himself as king. New victories made him, for a few years, the most powerful man in Europe. But in 1812 his invasion of Russia went terribly wrong and his empire began to crumble. By 1815 he was finished. For Italy, this meant a return to Austrian rule.

Napoleon used Italy for his own advantage, adding large areas to France and recruiting Italians for his armies. But his rule also showed Italians the benefits of a well-run government. And, by creating the short-lived Kingdom of Italy, Napoleon revived the idea of Italy as a nation.

Napoleon at Arcola
by Antoine-Jean Gros (1771–1835). This painting is in the Napoleon Museum at Arenenberg, Switzerland.

Gros was Napoleon's official battle painter. His job was to make Napoleon's wars seem great and glorious – and he was so good at it that Napoleon made him a baron! Here, Napoleon is shown carrying the battle standard on the bridge at Arcola, where his action is said to have put new heart into the French army.

ITALIANS IN REVOLT

By the early nineteenth century, many Italians had become determined to drive out their foreign masters. Yet, in spite of plots and rebellions all over the country, the Austrians and their allies always proved too strong.

Manin Proclaims the Venetian Republic
by an unknown artist. It is in the Correr Museum, Venice. Daniele Manin, led the Venetian rebellion against Austrian rule.

After the fall of Napoleon, the Austrians held down Italy with a heavy hand. In every Italian state the rulers were free to crush any opposition. Government spies were everywhere, making it dangerous to speak freely, and people were not allowed to publish books or writings that criticized the ruling powers.

Italians who wanted to change things joined secret societies, which supported uprisings in many parts of Italy during the 1820s and 1830s. When these revolts failed, Giuseppe Mazzini (1805–72), who had been exiled from Italy, founded an organization called Young Italy. Mazzini's calls for a national revolution and a united Italy had great influence. Slowly the idea spread that Italy must be free.

In 1848 revolution came at last almost everywhere in Europe, including Austria. The people of Milan and Venice took advantage of the situation to drive out the Austrians. Under pressure from his subjects, King Charles Albert of Piedmont reluctantly agreed to help Milan, but he acted too slowly and was beaten by the Austrians.

Milan fell, but Venice held out. In February 1849, Rome was captured by Italian revolutionary forces. Mazzini and a brilliant amateur soldier, Giuseppe Garibaldi (1807–82), were among the leaders. When a French army was sent against them, they defended the city bravely but were finally forced to give in. When, in August 1849, Venice surrendered to the Austrians, Italy's bid for freedom came to an end.

Giuseppe Garibaldi
by Girolamo Induno (1827–90). The picture is in the Risorgimento Museum, Turin.

Garibaldi became the great military leader the Italians needed in their fight for freedom.

TOWARDS A UNITED ITALY

The revolutions in Italy failed to drive out the Austrians. The prime minister of Piedmont, Count Camillo Cavour, realized that the only way to succeed was to ask for help from foreign countries.

In the 1850s Piedmont seemed to be Italy's last hope. Piedmont was an Italian state with an Italian army and had helped the revolutionaries in 1848. Since then, it had established a parliamentary system of government. Prime Minister Cavour was very clever and cautious. He did not hope to unite all of Italy at once, but to strengthen Piedmont and get rid of the Austrians. He worked hard to win the support of France, which was believed to have the best army in Europe. Finally, in 1858, he persuaded the French emperor, Louis Napoleon, to make an alliance with Piedmont.

In April 1859, Cavour lured the Austrians into declaring war. The French and Piedmontese won victories at Magenta and Solferino, but the battles were much bloodier than Louis Napoleon had expected. Instead of driving the Austrians right out of Italy, he made peace, leaving them with Venezia, the region in the north-east surrounding Venice. However, Piedmont did gain Lombardy, a large Austrian province with its capital at Milan.

Once started, the drive towards Italian unity was hard to stop. Other parts of northern Italy rebelled and voted to join Piedmont. Louis Napoleon eventually agreed, but in return Piedmont had to give the provinces of Nice and Savoy to France. As Cavour had planned, Piedmont was greatly strengthened. The crisis seemed to be over.

A Cavalry Encounter during the Battle of Solferino, 24 June 1859 ▶
by Anton Hoffman. This painting is in a private collection.

▲ The artist was Austrian, so he shows the French cavalryman getting the worst of it. In reality, the French won the battle.

THE RISORGIMENTO

Cavour's policy had worked, but it was the bold revolutionary actions of Garibaldi that made it certain that Italy would become a nation. Italians proudly call the events of 1859–70 the Risorgimento – the Resurrection, or raising of the country from the dead.

The Embarkation of the Thousand from the Banks of the Quarto
by Pierre Tetar Van Elven (1828–1908). It belongs to the city of Genoa.

Gathering together a mere thousand volunteers, Garibaldi overthrew the Kingdom of Naples and Sicily.

A new phase of the Risorgimento began in May 1860, when Garibaldi set sail from Quarto, near Genoa, with a thousand volunteers. They landed in Sicily, beyond the reach of Piedmont and the great powers. Their goal was to overthrow the unpopular Bourbon king of Naples and Sicily and by doing so help the cause of Italian unity.

Garibaldi's tiny, red-shirted band defeated the king's troops and was soon joined by thousands of Sicilians who were discontented with Bourbon rule. In August, Garibaldi crossed to the mainland, and by 7 September he had entered the city of Naples.

The heroism of 'The Thousand' stirred all Italy and forced Cavour to act. Piedmontese troops invaded the Papal States, which separated the north from the south. All the Papal States were occupied, except the area around Rome, which was under French protection. Although Garibaldi would rather have seen Italy become a republic, he decided to hand over the south to the Piedmontese king, Victor Emmanuel II, who became the first king of Italy.

Although Italy now existed as a nation, Venezia and Rome were still in foreign hands. But in 1866, Italy gained Venezia after helping the German state of Prussia to defeat the Austrians. Then in 1870, France, faced by the increasingly strong Prussians, withdrew its troops from Rome. The Italians took their chance and marched in. The Risorgimento had been carried out.

◀ The painting makes it clear that 'The Thousand' are ordinary men who have chosen to fight for Italy. They are not soldier-like, but sit and stand about while they wait to set sail.

THE NEW ITALY

The new Italy faced many problems. The Italians had become the citizens of a single country, but they were deeply divided in many ways. And, by comparison with most European states, Italy remained poor and backward.

Italy had been united very quickly, and people from different regions found it hard to get used to working together. This weakened Italy's parliament and system of government. Another problem was that the pope remained angry with the new Italy because it had taken away his political power. On the pope's orders, many Catholics refused to take part in national affairs.

There was also great poverty in Italy, especially in the south. People there felt they had gained little from the Risorgimento, and for a long time Sicily was in a state of near-rebellion, held down by the Italian army. Poverty was made worse by a rapidly rising population. There were 22 million Italians in 1840, increasing to 40 million in 1915, even though several million others had left Italy to settle in countries such as the USA.

In the 1880s, Italy began to make industrial progress. The textile industry revived, and in 1899 a new machine – the car – began to be manufactured by Fiat and later by other firms. About this time, trade unions and socialist parties appeared. They aimed to improve workers' conditions and to change society. But violence between striking workers and the police and army caused great bitterness.

Italy was not really a great power, but its leaders tended to forget the fact. Some even believed that a war would be a good thing because it would unite the country. But the reality of war was to show how wrong they were.

▼ *The Advance of the Fourth Estate*
by Giuseppe Pellizza da Volpedo
(1868–1907). It is in the Gallery of
Modern Art, Milan.

The Fourth Estate means ordinary
working people, as opposed to the
other three estates (groups) of
aristocracy, clergy and the rich.

◀ These farm workers are
shown coming out on
strike. By painting them
marching towards us,
the artist makes them
seem heroic and strong.

THE FIRST WORLD WAR

The First World War of 1914–18 was a terrible conflict that cost millions of lives. Italy took part on the winning side, but the Italian people suffered greatly.

The Charge of the Lancers
by Umberto Boccioni (1882–1916),
It is in the Brera Gallery, Milan.

Boccioni was one of the Futurist artists who glorified war and energy. He died during the First World War.

The war broke out in August 1914 between the Central Powers (Germany and Austria-Hungary) and the Entente or Allies (France, Russia and Britain). Italy had strong links with the Central Powers, but wisely decided to stay out of the conflict. But some Italians were eager to enter the war, either to unify the Italian people or for gain or glory.
A number of leading writers and artists of the time, called the Futurists, even glorified war and machinery; the

painting *The Charge of the Lancers* gives an idea of the heroic energy that the Futurists so much admired.

All the same, most Italians were against going to war. But in April 1915, Italy's leaders made a secret deal with the Allies. The British and French agreed that, if Italy fought on their side, it would be rewarded with Austrian territories that the Italians claimed were theirs. Italy declared war and attacked Austria-Hungary.

The Italians fought the war on the slopes of the Alps, but all their attacks failed. In October 1917, the Italian army suffered a shattering defeat at Caporetto. The Allied powers sent help, and the Italians managed to hold on. Then, gradually, the war in France turned against the Central Powers, and by late 1918 they were on the point of collapse. In October 1918, the Italian armies began a general advance which forced the Austrians to ask for peace. The war ended in victory for Italy and its allies, but the price – 600,000 Italian lives – had been very high.

Boccioni's painting shows the mad ▷ confusion of horses, men, lances and rifles very effectively. But the First World War itself was far bloodier than anything the Futurists had imagined.

MUSSOLINI AND FASCISM

The 1920s and 1930s were a troubled period when many countries fell under the control of dictators. Italy became one of the first countries to be ruled by a dictator when Benito Mussolini and his Fascist Party seized power.

The First World War unsettled the Italians. Many felt that the parliamentary system of government had failed. They blamed the government for the fact that Italy gained little from the war and for the high unemployment after the war. Angry workers often demonstrated, went on strike and took over factories. Such actions raised people's hopes, or fears, that there would be a socialist revolution.

Fear of revolution helped the new Fascist movement, founded in 1919 by Benito Mussolini (1883–1945). The Fascists organized themselves into units, as in an army, and beat up and sometimes killed their opponents – mostly the socialists. Many wealthy and powerful people sympathized with the Fascists, and the weakness of the Italian government encouraged the Fascists to try to take power. On 28 October 1922, they made a famous march on the capital, Rome. The Fascists were not really strong, but no one stood up to them. The government resigned and Mussolini became prime minister. Over the next few years, all opposition parties were crushed and Italy became a Fascist country with Mussolini as dictator.

▲ Roman officials carried bundles of rods, called *faces*. Mussolini's Fascist Party took its name from these symbols of the state.

Fascism was based on militarism and hero-worship of the leader. But military parades and speeches failed to solve Italy's economic problems. Mussolini remained popular

Benito Mussolini
In this poster, the dictator appears in a uniform with medals and surrounded by symbols of Italian greatness.

with Italians when he attacked Ethiopia, an African country that was helpless against Italian bombs and poison gas. Ethiopia was added to Italy's empire.

Mussolini made an alliance with the German dictator, Adolf Hitler, who also followed aggressive policies. When Hitler's troops marched into Poland in September 1939, Britain and France declared war on Germany and the Second World War began. Now that Italy was Hitler's ally, what would Mussolini do?

THE END OF FASCISM

The Second World War showed up Italy's lack of real military power. Failures and defeats destroyed Fascism, and Italy's good name was saved only by the Italians who fought against the Fascists.

A scene from the film *Two Women*
directed by Vittorio De Sica
(1901–74).

The Italian film industry became very important towards the end of the Second World War. De Sica's film, starring Sophia Loren and Jean-Paul Belmondo, describes the suffering of a mother and daughter during this period.

In September 1939, Mussolini stayed out of the war, telling his German allies that Italy lacked the materials needed to fight. But a series of great German victories changed his mind. Mussolini decided to bring Italy in on Hitler's side to get a share of the spoils of war before it was all over.

This proved to be a fatal mistake. The war went on, and Italy suffered defeat after defeat. The Greeks drove back an Italian invasion of their country. The Italian empire in Africa was lost. Many Italians died in Russia, fighting alongside the Germans. Italy itself was bombed and finally, in July 1943, the country was invaded by British, American and allied forces.

By this time even the Fascists had had enough of Mussolini. He fell from power, and the new Italian government prepared to change sides in the war. But the Germans rushed in more troops, and for almost two years Italy suffered as the British, the Americans and their allies fought their way up from the south of the country.

Mussolini had been imprisoned, but the Germans rescued him and set up a Fascist state in the north – with the Germans holding the real power. Anti-Fascist Italians formed resistance groups, called partisans, to fight behind the lines. They managed to free a number of cities. Finally, as the last Germans and Fascists tried to escape, Mussolini was caught and shot by partisans on 28 April 1945. A few days later the war ended.

With the Eighth Army on the Sangro, November 1943
by Edward Ardizzone (1900–79). This picture is in the Imperial War Museum, London.

The artist has sketched British and Allied troops resting in a village near the River Sangro in central Italy. Almost two years of fierce fighting in Italy caused great suffering.

MODERN ITALY

After the war, Italy shared in the growing prosperity of western and central Europe. But political failures and north–south differences continued to cause problems. Even in the 1990s, Italy still faced serious difficulties.

In 1946, Italians voted to get rid of the king and have a republic. Italy became a full democracy in which all adult citizens could vote. The war left the country in ruins and recovery was slow until about 1958, when the economy greatly improved. Italy also benefited by joining the European Common Market (now the European Union, or EU).

By the 1960s, most Italians enjoyed a high standard of living, owning cars, refrigerators and televisions. Politically as well as economically, Italy was part of the Western world, belonging to the American-led NATO alliance. Like other countries, Italy suffered from problems such as terrorism – acts of violence by small groups who hoped to overthrow the state. The terrorists were particularly active in the 1970s, but were finally defeated in the early 1980s.

The Ferrari Testarossa
The quality of Italian design is admired throughout the world – from fashion to cars.

This high-quality 1988 model is typical of the Italian motor industry. During its long history, Italian car-makers have produced outstanding family, luxury and racing cars.

Italian high fashion ▶
Italy is one of the world leaders in fashion. This 1995 evening gown, with its striking red and white checks, is the work of the famous designer Gianni Versace.

Italians disliked their political system, in which government was based on deals between political parties, and government funds were used to buy votes. Old problems remained unsolved, including the poverty and crime that still existed in the south. The power of the criminal organization known as the Mafia, founded in Sicily, was so great that officials who investigated it were frequently murdered.

In 1992, it was revealed that many of Italy's political and business leaders were taking or giving bribes. Because of these scandals, some political parties collapsed and important changes were made in the way parliament was elected. The future was, as always, uncertain.

GLOSSARY

Alliance An agreement between countries to co-operate and come to each other's aid. They are known as allies.

Barbarian General name used by the ancient Greeks and Romans for people living outside their civilization.

Bishop A high-ranking member of the priesthood.

Bribes Money or other gifts offered to encourage someone to do something illegal or morally wrong.

Carnival A time of feasting and merrymaking.

Civil war A war between groups of people who live in the same country.

Colony An area ruled by people from another country.

Counter-Reformation The movement to put new life into the Roman Catholic Church and combat the Reformation (see below).

Democratic Describes a political system of rule in which the government has been freely elected by the people. This type of government is called a democracy.

Dictator A leader of a country who has absolute, or complete, power.

Empire A group of countries or territories governed by the same ruler.

Exile To force a person to leave his or her own country.

Fascist Someone who believes in fascism, an anti-democratic political movement founded by Mussolini.

Fasting Avoiding food for a certain period of time, often for religious reasons.

Import To bring goods in from another country.

Militarism An outlook that glorifies making war and conquests.

Monastery A place where monks and friars live.

NATO North Atlantic Treaty Organization – the North American and western European alliance, in existence since 1949.

Parliament The assembly of people who make the laws of a country.

Peninsula A long strip of land surrounded by the sea on three sides.

TIMELINE

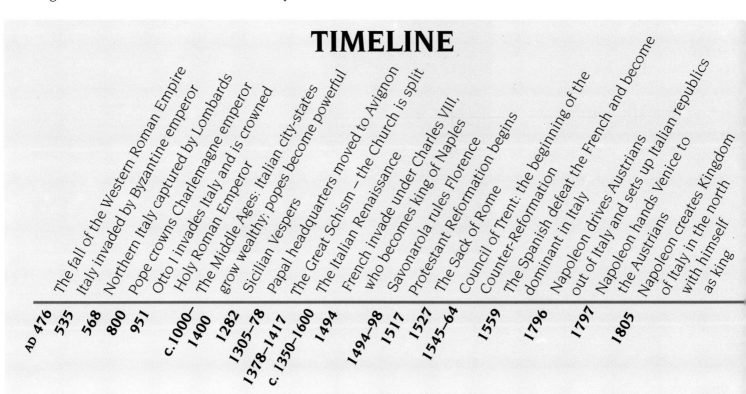

AD 476 — The fall of the Western Roman Empire
535 — Italy invaded by Byzantine emperor
568 — Northern Italy captured by Lombards
800 — Pope crowns Charlemagne emperor
951 — Otto I invades Italy and is crowned Holy Roman Emperor
c.1000–1400 — The Middle Ages: Italian city-states grow wealthy; popes become powerful
1282 — Sicilian Vespers
1305–78 — Papal headquarters moved to Avignon
1378–1417 — The Great Schism – the Church is split
c.1350–1600 — The Italian Renaissance
1494 — French invade under Charles VIII, who becomes king of Naples
1494–98 — Savonarola rules Florence
1517 — Protestant Reformation begins
1527 — The Sack of Rome
1545–64 — Council of Trent: the beginning of the Counter-Reformation
1559 — The Spanish defeat the French and become dominant in Italy
1796 — Napoleon drives Austrians out of Italy and sets up Italian republics
1797 — Napoleon hands Venice to the Austrians
1805 — Napoleon creates Kingdom of Italy in the north with himself as king

Philosopher A thinker who studies basic questions about life and knowledge.

Politician Someone holding or seeking to hold a position in the government.

Reformation The sixteenth-century religious movement that aimed to reform the Roman Catholic Church and resulted in the foundation of Protestant churches.

Reforming Bringing about change.

Republic A nation in which the head of state is an elected president, not a king or queen.

Revolution The overthrow of a government, usually by violent means.

Roman Catholic Church One of the Christian churches, headed by the pope in Rome.

Saints People whose great holiness is recognized by the Church.

Socialist Someone who believes in socialism. Its main idea is that the people, not individuals, should own a country's wealth.

Trade union An organization of workers that aims to protect the interests of its members.

Volunteer A person who takes up a task, for example joining an army, of his or her own free will.

BOOKS TO READ

History of Art for Young People by H.W. Janson (Thames and Hudson, 1989)

Italian Heritage Dictionary ed. Pierre Rengi (Magi Publications, 1990)

Renaissance Art by Nathaniel Harris (Wayland, 1994)

Western Art 1600-1800 by Christopher McHugh (Wayland, 1994)

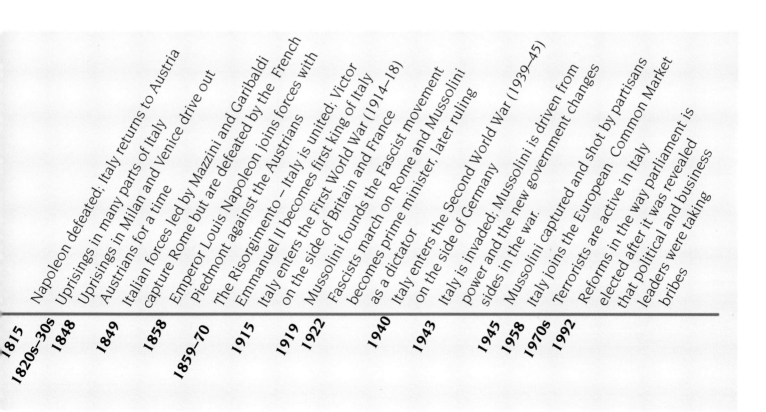

1815	Napoleon defeated: Italy returns to Austria
1820s-30s	Uprisings in many parts of Italy
1848	Uprisings in Milan and Venice drive out Austrians for a time
1849	Italian forces led by Mazzini and Garibaldi capture Rome but are defeated by the French
1858	Emperor Louis Napoleon joins forces with Piedmont against the Austrians
1859-70	The Risorgimento – Italy is united: Victor Emmanuel II becomes first king of Italy
1915	Italy enters the First World War (1914–18) on the side of Britain and France
1919	Mussolini founds the Fascist movement
1922	Fascists march on Rome and Mussolini becomes prime minister, later ruling as a dictator
1940	Italy enters the Second World War (1939–45) on the side of Germany
1943	Italy is invaded: Mussolini is driven from power and the new government changes sides in the war.
1945	Mussolini captured and shot by partisans
1958	Italy joins the European Common Market
1970s	Terrorists are active in Italy
1992	Reforms in the way parliament is elected after it was revealed that political and business leaders were taking bribes

INDEX